Loose Marbles and Pretty Words

To Die and Live Again in Los Angeles

Evan Raiff

Loose Marbles and Pretty Words:

To Die and Live Again in Los Angeles Copyright © 2023, Evan Raiff

Illustrated By: Scott Milton Brazee
Formatted By: Bhavnish Kumar

ISBN: 979-8-9880493-0-2 (paperback)

Contents

Letter From the Author

Hello Dear Reader,

We only get so much time on this rock, so thank you for spending some of it on my words and thoughts. This book is the purging of a downward spiral and a triumphant return to oneself. It is my love letter to Los Angeles and a shriek into the void of eternity. Hopefully that sums it up well.

Before continuing forward, please be warned that there are some dark and sensitive subjects discussed and written about. If, at any point, the writing triggers or makes you uncomfortable, put the book down, step away, and breathe. The intent of this book is to express the soul, not harm the mind.

I hope to make this journey worth your while. You deserve nothing less. The only thing I will ask of you is to allow whatever emotions this book inspires to be what they are. Feel them fully, embrace them, do not judge them before they bloom.

And if this book inspires nothing, then it makes an excellent paperweight.

Thank you again, Dear Reader.

Evan

40: *Loose Marbles*

If the map were made of marbles
And each of us a sphere
Tilting the map would only loosen a small portion

Most would stay where they are
Or perhaps move a few inches
But they would gladly hold their place

The others
The rest of us
Would gather and collect
In the bottom left
And huddle together for warmth in a cold city that
is melted by the desert sun

We all flock to this land
At the beck and call of the angels
Some for safety
Others for dreams
But each of us with purpose

Cracked
Chipped
Uneven marbles
Rolling along the dirt

Until we find our home in the desert sand

50: Green Thumb, Crimson Palms

A flower such as this should not bloom in the desert
Yet here you stand
Glimmering in the sunlight

Your petals twirling and spiraling as they fall
Bursting to flame as they settle in the scorching sand
Until only ash remains

The fleeting shade you provide
Lasts long enough to leave a lingering taste
So sweet it forms an addiction

Shades of red and pink hues
Dazzling across your sunset petals
Accented by pearly white sadness

In any other part of the world
This desert rose would wither and die
Yet here it stands

Clogged roots nourished by travelers
who stayed too long
Swallowed and consumed by isolation

I will hold you close, my sweet desert rose
And our thorns can bury themselves into one another

44: Lemonade as Sweet as Sisyphus

The sweet smell of heavenly nectar
The citrus ichor presented to every golden cow
It was so close

But now your boulder is at the bottom of a hill

Again

The angels sing from the mountaintop
Promises of glory and triumph
Begging for one more try

Just as they did after your last failure

The lemons that grow in abundance
Are not the most bitter fruit of this desert garden

This city consumes you whole
Every ounce
In every way
Until the day
It decides you are worthy

But even a chance is enough

Perhaps this try will be different
If not, this torture is better than the alternative

And as we strain to push our boulder upwards
We revel in the untamable bitterness
Of this sun blessed plastic lemon grove

41: Sonder

The glittering stars sparkle and shine above
As headlight and midnight oil lamps
Glimmer and wave in the rising smog

All I can see are people I may never meet
Each one a separate collection of dreams, wants,
fears, and desires
Each one existing

Existing

Somehow, in a city of millions
We are all strangers

We isolate within cheap apartments
We hide behind dashboards
Keeping our legs treading just under the surface
of the pond
So we do not drown in the loneliness of this city

We cast off our humanity for the chance to fly
On wings made from cheap wax
And held together by thrifted shoestrings

I want to know all of it
Every moment
Of every life

Collected in the Book of Us
If not to share then at least for myself

So I can read it in the cold desert night
As I fall asleep to another freeway lullaby

54: LA Drivers

His horn blared until his car collided with mine
Futile honking in a last-ditch warning

His brakes failed
And I couldn't merge fast enough in this traffic

Now we sit on the side of the road
As the horde of metallic chariots race by

He soothes his crying daughter in a tongue
I don't understand
He apologizes with the voice of a father who is
scared, not angry

Passersby break their necks
To observe the mundane
Craving the suffering of others
Hoping for a story to distract from their own

One yells obscenities at the man
Emboldened by the anonymity the faceless
mass provides

The damage is minimal
Four wheels and an engine
More shaken than scarred

Both of us are unharmed
Nothing could be more important than that

With a handshake and reassurance
We go our separate ways
Never to meet again

Meshing back into the metallic herd
Rejoining the other fish swimming upstream

Becoming another set of indistinguishable faces
Trying to get home during rush hour

12: *Gray Eyed Nomad*

The world passes by you on all sides
Rushing there and nowhere
Rats racing in every direction

Yet you are still
Hands outstretched
Relying on kindness in an unkind world
Rejecting the poison they call help

They would seek to take your freedom, wouldn't they?
They would force you into the frenzy
Pulled there and nowhere
Shaved down to a mindless drone

You are not meant for that

You were born to wander, weren't you,
gray eyed nomad?
Those once bright eyes meant to see the world
Now you may, on your terms
Should you find the means to do so

You are free while they remain chained

Sheep criticizing the wounded,
refuse covered pigeon
Only one can fly away

They will scorn you
Beat you
Curse you

For you have seen that the figures on the
wall are merely shadows
And they are forced to return to the cave
from whence you escaped

46: 100% Organic, Non-GMO Plastic

As the vagabond blares his instrument
Lonely trumpet whispers of melancholy desires
The spirit of destiny manifests

How can you not love this city?

So full of potential
For the creation of art
For the destruction of your soul

This beautiful calm lake
With flailing bodies drowning just under the surface

Where independence is the latest trend
As the machine churns and burns
The ideals and hopes of those it inspired

The beautiful people
So full of vibrancy and ambition
Apathetic to the thoughts of strangers if it will
grab their attention

These buzzwords given flesh
Golden, sparkling mannequins
The envy of everyone else's eyes

This city is beautiful plastic
Formed and reformed every day

We worship at the altar of this blessed hellscape
Drinking from the drains of promised glory
In hopes that we too will become plastic

This city
Twisted veneer and facade of happiness

How can you not fall in love with it?

5: *Scars*

We are all covered in scars
Pretending they do not exist

That we are flawless,
Perfect

Yet, the scars are always there
Inside

Reminders of who we once were
The pain of stretching and growing to
Become

Whole
Complete
People

There is no growth without pain
But we seek the comfort of who we were
Being told the only way to grow
Is to never change

Silly

The only way to grow
As humans

Is to pick the scabs

And bleed

16: Steaming Crucibles and Ocean Flames

I offer myself as tribute
To be thrown to the fire as kindling

Let my soul be the spark that ignites the pyre

Let my blood become a wave of words to
drown the world

My bones remain
To stoke the flame
Of a forge beneath the waves

A furnace burning at the depths of the
Mariana trench
Heat-soaked innards steaming, fuming
Consuming
Until ashes remain beneath the foam

The maddening hammering within the temple of bone
Forging endless cascades of literature and syllables

To bring drink to a parched world

To spill rain upon the desert

Let the flame consume me whole
And may the brine preserve what is left

67: Writer's Block

I keep waiting for something amazing
A flash of inspiration
But all
I see
Is a blinking line
On a blank page
Ticking away the seconds
Of another wasted day

15: Faith, Trust, and Pixie Dust

If you be so lucky, shut your eyes and watch
Bright and flashing colors!
Shapes and sounds galore!

Now squint
And hold your breath
Those colors are so bright they must be on fire!

So long as you believe

The lights grow dim with each passing moment
Darkened by the burden of growing up

It will come for us all, the passage of time
Dancing yellow eyes of the crocodile
Tick, tock, tick, tock

You will be told to grow up, little canvas
Cowardice in the guise of bravery
Unable to combat the ever-spinning wheel of time

Remember your cleverness, little canvas
Do not forget you can fly
Two stars to the left and until morning

Continue to believe, little canvas
Do not say goodbye

Goodbye means going away
Going away means forgetting how to fly

Please do not forget, little canvas
Please do not let the colors fade, little canvas

Once they do, they are gone forever

28: *The Sin of Being Human in the Presence of Angels*

They do not falter in their stride
They do not weep in dark corners of their room

It's so easy for them
It's so easy for everyone

There must be something wrong with me

Brown eyes, behind blue hues of sadness, watch
with frenzied envying green
As they soar and ascend
Pristine wings gleaming in the sunlight

All I have are crumbs of once giant endeavors
But no one in this city eats bread

Wings are given when the bell rings
And I only hear it toll

But if that is all I hear
Then I must pierce the dirt and dig

Somewhere between heart and soul
Between was and will be
I must dig

Either I will unearth something long forgotten
Or save the gravedigger a day's work

49: And yet...

I have someone who loves me
Food on my plate
Friends to share my world with
A family in support of a pipe dream

And yet...

The whispers keep me awake
Anxieties claw at early morning thoughts
Depression tears at late evening hopes
Misery festers within my arteries

I checked every box
Completed every assignment
Exactly as recommended

One step into the next
Feet placed exactly within the outlines
Of the millions of footsteps that came before
I followed the path perfectly

And yet...

I am lost

26: Fool King of a Forest of Dreams

We were promised kingdoms in our youth
Kings and Queens of fulfilled dreams
Ruling over lands of untapped potential

What a curse to lay upon a child

The world was our oyster
if our heart and mind were set
But hearts cannot harvest
And minds cannot shuck

Having the potential for anything
Means being potentially everything
Dreams become binding when they twist
into uncertain knots

This dark desert forest has many paths
New dreams appearing each day
Venturing down fresh and exciting trails
To exactly where I was when I started

The shimmering light of gold stars
Cannot pierce the thick canopy of
overwhelming indecision
A pat on the back cannot point which way to turn

I was supposed to be anything
But I wished to be everything

And now I perch on the branches of indecision
Unsure of which noose is best

37: *A Sample of the Love Letters My Demons Write Me at Sunset*

Four peaceful walls built by your own sweat and tears
Loving faces lavishing adoration
Fledgling success kindling hopes and a dream

You don't deserve this

You haven't earned it

You can lie to everyone else
And they will believe it

But
I know you
All of you
And we both know
The disappointment you truly are

One day they'll find out
One day they'll see through the lies

That you are not who they think you are
A swindler, a selfish thief of their precious moments

They waste their love and appreciation
On filth like you

If you really cared for them
You'd leave them alone

Tethering yourself to loved ones
So you have company while you drown
What sort of monster would do such a thing?

Ignore me all you want
Bury your head in the sand
Temporary distractions can only silence me for so long

You have to go to bed eventually
And I love our nightly pillow talk

1: Dear God, Change the Channel and I'll Believe in You Again

I can't watch

Two billion

Three hundred and ninety-six million

Seven hundred and thirty-six thousand

Seconds

Of this

Of work, chores, sleep
Repeat
Forever

It's the same episode as yesterday

There was supposed to be more
They told me there would be more

The remote batteries are dead
And all
I have left is tomorrow
It's the same episode as every day
Again

And Again

58: No Vacancy Within an Empty Home

I sent them away
My inner demons
My dearest friends

In their stead
A new stranger has moved in

Quiet, elusive
Only glimpsing him for a moment
In the shattered reflection of a broken mirror

We have the same face
Except for when I look into his eyes

He is at peace
While I continue to wage war upon myself

The grinning chatter of anxiety
The dampening weight of depression
Both sent off to dwell anywhere else but here

In their absence
The silence is deafening
And I no longer know myself

Show me the way, familiar stranger
Let me see what parts of my soul they
took when they left

18: I Buried My Dad When I Was Sixteen but His Reflection Haunts Me Every Day

In a city of vapid reflection
The almighty mirror speaks no lies

It falls upon us to accept them
And not hate the glass for it

The angels sing of wondrous escape
72 hymns of promised peace
Of freedom from the shackles

To outrun the pacing demons unleashed by those we
never met
Bearing down on us for generations

We ran west
Spurred on by youthful flame
And eager pettiness

To be different

But our hands are theirs,
Crafted by generations along the plains

Our heart is theirs,
The same drum they danced to by the fireside

Ancient times and lives past call out

To pry

Pry Into the past
Harvesting rotting branches from an old tree,
of which we are the most recent crop

Pry Into our homes
Ripping up poorly placed floorboards to meet the
monsters in the basement

Pry Into ourselves
Scattering pieces of heart and soul as we become the evils
we once hated

It happens to us all
In one way or another
We become the previous incarnation

As our offspring will become us

Rebellion to leader to loving, withered husk
The cycle continues
Time marches on
Painting a double helix tapestry

We become what we once spurned

We become what they once were

Did our parents want to be different, too?

38: To Offer an Apology Upon a Stranger's Grave

He never cared for flowers
But this was the best I had to give

He would have hated to be forgiven
But I wanted to apologize all the same

For every ambition he clutched
Squeezing and stretching it to a whip
So he could lash his own back

For the rhythmic hymn he moaned
A chorus of failure and doubt
To be sung to the crystal blue skies

For all the flashes of anger
Sudden and unpredictable roars
Of bellicose self-hatred spilling over

For his shattered knees
Broken and worn down
From refusing to share his burden

There were many who loved him
Despite his pride and flaws

But I am not among them

I stand in this cemetery
With a bouquet of words

To lament who

I once was

47: Sometimes I Miss the Cruelty

Wonderful smiles surround me on all sides
Kind words uttered at every instance
Unquestioned support from close friends

And the warm breeze softly kisses my neck
Barely a cloud to disrupt the waterless Eden
Time and seasons lost to constant paradise

But sometimes, it is hard not to miss the cold

Of the air

Of the people

Because that cold reveals your character
It humbles you, strips you of any facade
Falsities and niceties become liabilities
When frigid air stabs your lungs with every breath

There is no subtext to winter's wrath
Huddling with strangers for enough warmth to survive
this white frozen hell
Together
Warm hearts crafted in a shivering forge

Sometimes
I do miss the cold
If only for the certainty it brought
There was no time for questions or doubt
We were too busy shoveling driveways

61: Bastard Children of Stardust and Dreams

Call your mother
She misses you

You have been so busy
Trying to sit upon the throne of the world

That you have forgotten to sit at the dinner table
And help her clean the dishes

23: Desert Sand Sea Shanties of Times Long Gone

Do they think of me often?
As often as I think of them?

Do their lips curl to a smile when
I pass their recollection?
Does my name leave a bitter taste in their mouths?

Am I even missed?

I spend some nights gazing at the stars
Thinking of ships that I have passed by in the night

Pursuing warmer winds
Dreaming of the ship decks left behind
Ships far better suited to sail the frozen Atlantic
My vessel is better suited for warmer seas
I hope it is

Warmer fates can lead to freezing nights
When there is nothing but time to think

As I floated west
So many pieces of my heart were left behind

Whatever parts of me still remain in the cold
I hope they bring warmth in the winters

I hope they still remain
In the shattered pieces of memory we call the past

Forever is only so long, it seems

I measure the love I have felt
By the holes in my chest

What a fortunate curse to have a Swiss cheese heart

31: (Stagnant) Water Under the (Old North) Bridge

This murky bog of darkened, lifeless water
It has not changed since I left it

Skinned knees still etched in the pavement
Tears still stain the ground
Painful whispers still linger on the wind

But there is warmth to be found within this swamp

The gnarled, twisting vines preserve
the faces of old friends
And we sip memories, savoring the familiarity
Finding hints of comfort in the legs of this wine
The grapes plucked just down the street

There is happiness to be found
Within the fog of this swamp
Such a shame it was not meant for me

But that doesn't mean
I can't come home
From time to time

24: Porciúncula

This muffled narrow stream,
entrapped in concrete gutters
This shameful relic, a mighty river
reduced to a sickly trickle

On rainy days a few drops will wake
it from its slumber
The brook overflows and
rages forth in unrelenting torrents

Finding a purpose in the rain

Bubbling froth bursts forth
Blessed by the few brash clouds that breach the blue
desert sky

A mighty river lives once more
All that was needed was water

Gray skies always light the way

57: Art is the Science of Cheating Death

Fulfillment in a full filament
Of the narrative plots that will earn me a plot

Dreaming of the holes I will leave
When I leave life in a hole

Shooting for the moon
To put my name in a star

So tourists can trample me while on vacation
And the next generation of artists can make music with
my bones

What a way to spend the days above ground

29: Green Pilgrimage to the Center of a Soul

I caught glimpses of him
In the rising smoke of a burning palm tree
And I thought I knew his face

I saw him for another moment
Between the unusual rain drops that are strangers here
And I recognized his smile

Now I stand before a regal hart
And in the black void of those buck's eyes
I see him once more

He tells me he is an old friend
One I had lost some time ago
But that he had never forgotten

He silences me before I speak
Whispers, "*Listen to the silence*"

As the sounds of chatter and fluorescent tubes fade away
The temple of verdant green wraps its vines around me

At last, I can see his features clearly

The stag turns and continues down its own path
Until it disappears into the woods
And he disappears again

I cannot tell if I have begun to slumber
Or awoken

But in this waking dream
I have found myself once more

3: Through the Thin-Paned Window Glass

This freedom comes at a price
Padded prison cells paid for out of pocket
Gouged paycheck to paycheck
Yet we stay

This tinsel covered wonderland
We all must be a little mad here

We could leave wonderland if we wished
And return to yesterday
I was a different person then
I wish to never be them again

But I miss the silence
The whispers of the stars
Communing with the crickets
What are they saying now?
All I can hear are the rumblings of airplanes through
glass as thin as paper

Craving silence in a wonderland of noise
Seeking inner peace in a piece of the world
Where tranquility is put upon a pedestal
Like a lamb to slaughter

Have I gone mad?

Yet every now and then I find it
It ceases to run and we sit beneath the tree
Nuzzling on the white rabbit's fur
In Silence
Stillness
Peace

These moments remind me
Why I came
Why I stay

The rabbit will run off soon
It only stays sleeping in my lap for so long

And I will continue to give chase
Believing six impossible things before breakfast

The air is filled with smog
And at last, I can breathe

13: *Marching Forward Towards the Dawn with Only Rhythm to Light the Way*

Breathe in, breathe out
Do you hear it?

Close your eyes, count backwards from 100
Do you hear it now?

That thump, thumping
Pump, pumping
Life, Blood, through your veins?

Can you hear it through the scabs?
Can you hear it through the wounds?
It beats stronger from each failure

That inner war drum
Rhythm
By you, for you, you alone

That thumping
Pumping
Instrument of

Overcoming

I hope you can hear it now

It beats stronger every day
If you let it

Breathe in, breathe out
Let the rhythm guide you towards the light

51: Romancing the Ephemeral Now

I never know the good times until the
moment has passed
Feeling my heart break as I leave
Like a one-night stand with a soulmate

The intimate embrace of the infinite now
Its passing is cause for celebration

Don't weep for this fleeting tender moment
Call me a cab of gratitude
Pay for the fare with time and love
Offer a parting kiss of remembrance

And when

I catch that perfume upon the wind
Those floral aromas of love with hints of kinship
and memory

I will hold the good times close again
For as long as they would have me

14: Lovin' Spoonful, Track 1

My youth was spent in far off lands
In the company of great heroes
Terrible villains, fearsome magic

Hoping beyond hope
Wishing beyond wish
That I would journey forth
My heroic deeds eternally retold

But the years went on
The magic faded

And sooner or later I gave up on the dream that
I am a prodigy

But in my budding wisdom
I found magic hidden within this mundane world

It is small
Delicate
But it is there

Tense muscles of intertwined hands
Howling laughter of early morning memories
The gravel in her voice as she whispers, 'Good morning'
In the simple act of being human

There is magic in the very word

Human

Once you look for it
It is impossible to miss

Little moments of humanity
Sacred moments of love

That is where the magic lives

17: Mountaintop Revelations of Ivory Boneyards

The dominoes fall in unfamiliar patterns
But still a form you built

The budding wisdom of age blooms
As youthful flowers wilt

What a world this is
That when all of it goes wrong

We can triumph, we can love
We can sing misery's happy song

Those wildly imperfect times
Every sunset that never happened

They shape us without knowing
Leading to places ne'er imagined

Each mistake a step
Up the mountainside of life

One at a time, that's all it is
When you journey through the night

As the bright sun rises
And the plateau spreads before you

Take a breath, take it in
Sit for a moment or two

You may rest here a while
You may choose to forge ahead

Perhaps there is another path
For you to climb instead

You do not know where your journey ends
But you will end up somewhere

That is the thrill of being alive
And I cannot wait to get there

35: Cuchulain Died Fighting the Ocean with a Smile on His Face

How beautiful is human nature
To scream into the void
Hoping the echoes will not fade
Laughing at the inevitable

As the birds build nests
And bees build hives
We build sandcastles upon the shore

Each day brings a new tide
One day our efforts will be washed away

Yet we build
We must build

We shout to the stars
Ripping our throats to tell the universe of our existence

Saying to the stars, '*I am here. Please don't forget me.*'

On this tiny blue pebble
In an ocean of gaseous nothing

Eventually, our skin wrinkles
Hairs grow gray

And as we fade into the black
The stars whisper back,

'*You were here. And you were beautiful.*'

Acknowledgments

To my family, for supporting these wild endeavors in one way or another. For raising me. For loving me.

To my friends, for shaping me and making this journey worthwhile. For the laughter, the lessons, and the memories.

To the SOBs, Up a Dae Dae.

To the people I no longer am close with, I hope you are doing well. We may not be at the same table anymore but I hope your plate is full.

To the many forges that crafted me.

To Bhavnish, for taking these pages and shaping them into something beautiful with your formatting.

To Scott, for taking these words and making them into something more with your illustrations.

To My Little Windmill, none of this is possible without you.

And to you, Dear Reader. For spending some of your few precious moments on a kid from a small town in Massachusetts who wound up in a Big City of Angels

About the Author

Evan Raiff is a Los Angeles based writer, actor, and producer. This is his first foray into poetry and his first poetry book, with aspirations to write more. He can be reached on Instagram at @evan_raiff or by email at eraiffmgmt@gmail.com.